ODIN, THE ALLFATHER.

ASGARD STORIES

ASGARD STORIES

TALES FROM NORSE MYTHOLOGY

BY

MARY H. FOSTER

AND

MABEL II. CUMMINGS, A.B.

ILLUSTRATED

ISBN: 978-93-5128-747-6(HB)

First Published in 1901
Indian Reprint in 2017

Published by

Kalpaz Publications
C-30, Satyawati Nagar,
Delhi – 110052
E-mail: kalpaz@hotmail.com
Website: kalpazpublications.com
Ph.: +91-9212142040

Cataloging in Publication Data—DK
Courtesy: D.K. Agencies (P) Ltd. <docinfo@dkagencies.com>

Foster, Mary H., author.
Asgard stories : tales from Norse mythology / by Mary H. Foster and Mabel H. Cummings (A.B).
pages cm
Reprint. Originally published: New York : Silver, Burdett and Company, 1901.
ISBN 9789351287476

1. Mythology, Norse. 2. Eddas. I. Cummings, Mabel H., author. II. Title.

PZ8.1.F815A84 2017 DDC 398.2 23

PREFACE.

This little volume is the outcome of several years' experience in telling to classes of children the classic myths, both southern and northern. The insight and interest displayed by the children encourage the authors to hope that other teachers and pupils may enjoy the myths here reproduced.

The interest shown at present in the teaching of myths to children seems to call for some such simple volume, giving the Norse myths in suitable form for use with pupils as well as for the children's home reading. There are various collections of the Greek tales, but the books dealing with the Norse myths seem to be more or less cumbered with detail, and, therefore, not adapted to very young readers.

The experience of the authors satisfies them that the teaching of myths should begin with those of the North, and that the Greek tales should be given later, with comparisons and references to the Norse myths. The stories which were dear to our own northern forefathers stir our children more deeply and are more congenial to them than those which come down to us from the Greeks. This is perfectly reasonable. The graphic descriptions in the Norse tales of the hard struggle with rugged nature and the severe climate of the North naturally come home more closely to us than the less rigorous and sturdy conditions of the southern nations. Then, too, the moral tone of the Norse myths is higher, purer, and more steadfast than that of the Greek tales, and is more congenial to our Teutonic point of view.

Much depends, of course, upon the teacher's careful study of the myths and insight into their significance. They should be presented in such manner as to awaken the interest of the children and lead them to make use of their own imagination.

The value of the Norse myths has been urged by Carlyle, Dasent, Anderson, and others. "To me there is in the Norse system something very genuine, very great, and manlike," wrote Carlyle. "A broad simplicity, so very different from the light gracefulness of the old Greek paganism, distinguishes this Norse system. It is thought, the genuine thought of deep, rude, earnest minds, fairly opened to the things about them, — a face-to-face and heart-to-heart inspection of things, — the first characteristic of all good thought in all times."

Anderson, the author of "Norse Mythology," wrote: "In the Norse mythology the centralizing idea is its peculiar feature; in it lies its strength and beauty. The one myth and the one divinity is inextricably in communion with the other; and thus also the idea of unity, centralization, is a prominent feature and one of the chief characteristics of the Teutonic nations.

"While the Greek mythology foreshadowed the petty states of Greece and southern Europe, the Norse mythology foreshadowed the political and social destinies of *United* Scandinavia, *United* Great Britain, and the *United* States of North America. . . .

"The poetic period of the child's own race should be melted and moulded into poetry, touched by a spark of Christian refinement and love, and then poured, so to speak, into his soul. The child's mind should feed upon the mythological stories and the primitive folk-lore of his race."

While many works have been consulted in the preparation of this volume, the authors are especially indebted to the following: Thorpe's translation of Sæmund's "Edda"; "The Younger Edda," in translations; Anderson's "Norse Mythology"; Guerber's "Myths of Northern Lands"; William and Mary Howitt's "Literature and Romance of Northern Europe"; and Mallet's "Northern Antiquities."

Brookline, Mass.,
September, 1901.

CONTENTS.

FULL-PAGE ILLUSTRATIONS.

THE STORY OF THE BEGINNING.

THE people who lived long ago, in the far-off lands of the north, watched the wonderful things that happened out of doors every day, just as we do; but they did not know about the one loving God, who is the Father of all, who made them and the world, and rules it by his wise laws; so they thought there must be a great many unseen powers, living in the clouds, in the wind, in the storms, and the sunshine, and doing all those wonders that no man could do.

And so those northern people, who were our own forefathers, came to believe in many gods — one for the sun, another for the thunder, another for the flowers, and so on.

In the long, dark winters, when the bright sun had gone away from them, these northmen had time to think many thoughts about the powers of frost, and wind, and storms, which they called giants, and they used to tell stories and sing songs about the short, bright summer, the thawing out of the streams and lakes, the coming of the birds and flowers.

With great joy the people saw the bright sun-god, Baldur, come back to them in the spring, after the long darkness, and knew that they owed their lives to his friendly warmth and light.

As we read the stories, or myths, told by those people long ago, we can see that they were meant to tell about the world around us. At first the stories were told and sung from father to son — that is, from one generation to another; but later, when people learned how to write, these myths were written down, and kept with great love and care.

This is the story they told of the Beginning. At first, before living creatures were in the world, it was all rough and without order. Far to the north it was very cold, for ice and snow were everywhere. Toward the south there was fire, and from the meeting of the fire and the cold a thick vapor was formed, from which sprang a huge giant. On looking about for some food, he saw a cow, who was also searching for something to eat. The ice tasted salt, and when the cow began to lick it, a head appeared, and at last the whole figure of a god stood before her.

From these two, the giant and the god, came the two great races of giants and gods, who were always enemies to each other. The giants were constantly trying to break into Asgard, the home of the gods, in the sky; the gods, on the other hand, watched and planned to keep out the giants, and to drive them back to their own stronghold, Utgard. Our world, where men and women lived, was between Utgard and Asgard; it was called Midgard, and around this Midgard world, under the ocean, was coiled a monstrous serpent, who grew so long that his tail grew down his throat. He was called the Midgard serpent.

A wonderful tree, named "Yggdrasil," connected all the worlds. This great ash tree had its roots in Utgard, and the tops of its branches reached up so high as to overshadow Asgard. Its three main roots were watered by three fountains, and near one of them sat the wise giant Mimir, of whom we shall hear later. The Norns, three sisters, also lived at the roots of Yggdrasil, and were careful to see that it was watered every day.

A little gray squirrel was always running up and down the tree, jerking his tail and hurrying to tell the news to every one along the way. He was so anxious to be the first one to carry the news, that many times he brought trouble to himself and to others, because he was not always careful to tell a story just as he had heard it, and often every one would have been happier if the squirrel had kept the story quite to himself.

The gods and goddesses, all together, were called the Æsir, and the chief and father of them all was Odin. His lofty throne rose high in the midst of Asgard, the sacred city, which the gods had built for their beautiful home.

From Asgard, arching over and down to the lower world, was a rainbow bridge, called Bifröst — "the trembling bridge"; upon this the dwellers in Asgard could travel every day, all except the mighty Thor. His thunder chariot was too heavy for "the trembling bridge," so he had to go around a longer way.

After the gods had made men and women, and had taught them to dwell on the earth, in the world of Midgard, Odin looked forth one morning from his heavenly seat, to see what further work was waiting for his helping hand.

He noticed, far away below him, a race of small beings, some of them busy, doing mischievous deeds, while others sat idle, doing nothing. Odin sent for all these little people to come to him, and when they had reached Asgard, and were admitted to his palace of Gladsheim, they entered the great judgment hall, where they found all the Æsir sitting, with Father Odin at their head.

The little people waited in a crowd near the door,

After the painting by Ehrenberg.

THE NORNS.

wondering what was going to happen to them, while Hermod, the messenger of the gods, ran to his master to say that they had come.

Then the Allfather spoke to the little dwarfs about their evil deeds among men, and he told the naughtiest ones that they must go and live down underground, and look after the great furnace fire in the middle of the earth, to keep it always burning. Some must get coal to feed the fire, and others still were to have charge of the gold, and silver, and precious stones, under the rocks. Not one of these busy dwarfs must ever appear during the day; only by night might they venture to leave their tasks.

"And now," said Odin, turning to the idle ones, "what have you been doing?"

"We were doing nothing at all, so we could not have harmed any one, and we pray you to spare us!" cried they.

"Do you not know that those who sit idle when they should be doing good deserve punishment, too?" said Odin. "I shall put you in charge of all the trees and flowers, and shall send one of the Æsir to teach you, so that you may be doing some good in the world."

Then the little elves went to work among the flowers, and Frey, the bright god of summer and sunshine, was a kind master to them. He taught them how to open the folded buds in the sunshine, to fill the honey cups, and lead the bees along the flower passages to find their food, to hatch the birds' eggs, and teach the little ones their songs, and then each night to fetch the water for dewdrops, to be hung on every leaf and blade of grass.

When their work was finished, and the moon had risen, these busy elves and fairies enjoyed many a happy evening, dancing and frisking on the green by moonlight. And so our world of Midgard was filled with busy work and play.

Even now, in our time, the people in the lands of the north, and in Germany, have many old sayings and stories that have come down to them from the days long ago. There is a beautiful white flower in the north, which is called Baldur's Brow, because it is so pure and bright, like the face of the dear sun-god, Baldur; and in some places, when the farmers gather in their harvest of grain, they leave a little bunch of it standing in the field, for Father Odin's horse.

We have some English names to remind us of those old tales of our forefathers, for we have Tuesday named for Tyr, or Tiu, the brave god who gave his right hand to save his friends; Wednesday, or Wodensday, named for Odin; Thursday, for Thor, the thunder-god; and Friday, for either the goddess Frigga, or Freyja, or for Frey, the god of summer, who ruled the fairies.

One night when all was quiet in Asgard and the Æsir had gone to rest, Odin, the Allfather, sat awake on his high throne, troubled with many thoughts. At his feet crouched his two faithful wolves, and upon his shoulders perched the two ravens of thought and memory, who flew far abroad every day, through the nine worlds, as Odin's messengers.

The Allfather had need of great wisdom in ruling the worlds; after thinking a long time on the matters which needed his care, he suddenly started up, and went forth with long strides from his palace of Gladsheim into the night. He soon returned, leading his beautiful, eight-footed steed, Sleipnir, and it was plain that Odin was going on a journey. He quickly mounted Sleipnir, and rode swiftly away toward Bifröst, the rainbow bridge, which reached from

Asgard, the city of the gods, down through the air to the lower worlds.

When Sleipnir stepped upon the bridge it trembled, and seemed hardly strong enough to bear the horse and his rider; but they had no fear of its giving way, and Sleipnir galloped swiftly onward.

Soon Odin saw Heimdall, the watchman of the bridge, riding toward him on a fine horse, with a golden mane that reflected light upon the noble face of his rider.

"You must be bound on some important errand, Father Odin, to be riding forth from Asgard so late at night," said Heimdall.

"It is indeed a most important errand, and I must hasten on," replied Odin. "It is well for us that we have such a faithful guardian of the 'trembling bridge'; if it were not for you, Heimdall, our enemies might long ago have taken Asgard by storm. You are so watchful, you can hear the grass grow in the fields, and the wool gather on the backs of the sheep, and you need less sleep than a bird. I myself stand in great need of wisdom, in order to take care of such faithful servants, and to drive back such wicked enemies!"

They hurried over the bridge until they came to Heimdall's far-shining castle, at the farther end of it. This was a lofty tower which was placed so as to guard the bridge, and it sent forth into the land of the giant enemies such a wonderful, clear light, that Heimdall could see, even in the darkest night, any one who came toward the bridge. Here Odin stopped a few moments to drink the mead which the good Heimdall offered him.

Then said Odin, "As I am journeying into the land of our enemies, I shall leave my good horse with you; there are not many with whom I would trust him, but I know that you, my faithful Heimdall, will take good care of him. I can best hide myself from the giants by going on as a wanderer."

With these words the Allfather quitted Heimdall's castle, and started off toward the north, through the land of the fierce giants.

During all the first day there was nothing to be seen but ice and snow; several times Odin was nearly crushed as the frost giants hurled huge blocks of ice after him.

The second day he came to mountains and broad rivers. Often when he had just crossed over a stream, the mountain giants would come after him to the other bank, and when they found that Odin had escaped them, they would send forth such a fierce yell, that the echoes sounded from hill to hill.

At the end of the third day, Odin came to a land where trees were green and flowers blooming.

Here was one of the three fountains which watered the world tree, Yggdrasil, and near by sat the wise giant, Mimir, guarding the waters of this wonderful fountain, for whoever drank of it would have the gift of great wisdom.

Mimir was a giant in size, but he was not one of the fierce giant enemies of the gods, for he was kind, and wiser than the wisest.

Mimir's well of wisdom was in the midst of a wonderful valley, filled with rare plants and bright flowers, and among the groves of beautiful trees were strange creatures, sleeping dragons, harmless serpents, and lizards, while birds with gay plumage flew and sang among the branches. Over all this quiet valley shone a lovely soft light, different from sunlight, and in the center grew one of the roots of the great world tree. Here the wise giant Mimir sat gazing down into his well.

Odin greeted the kind old giant, and said, "Oh, Mimir, I have come from far-away Asgard to ask a great boon!"

"Gladly will I help you if it is in my power," said Mimir.

"You know," replied Odin, "that as father of gods and men I need great wisdom, and I have come to beg for one drink of your precious water of knowledge. Trouble threatens us, even from one of the

Æsir, for Loki, the fire-god, has lately been visiting the giants, and I fear he has been learning evil ways from them. The frost giants and the storm giants are always at work, trying to overthrow both gods and men; great is my need of wisdom, and even though no one ever before has dared ask so great a gift, I hope that since you know how deep is my trouble, you will grant my request."

Mimir sat silently, thinking for several moments, and then said, "You ask a great thing, indeed, Father Odin; are you ready to pay the price which I must demand?"

"Yes," said Odin, cheerfully, "I will give you all the gold and silver of Asgard, and all the jeweled shields and swords of the Æsir. More than all, I will give up my eight-footed horse Sleipnir, if that is needed to win the reward."

"And do you suppose that these things will buy wisdom?" said Mimir. "That can be gained only by bearing bravely, and giving up to others. Are you willing to give me a part of yourself? Will you give up one of your own eyes?"

At this Odin looked very sad; but after a few moments of deep thought, he looked up with a bright smile, and answered, "Yes, I will even give you one of my eyes, and I will suffer whatever else is asked, in order to gain the wisdom that I need!"

We cannot know all that Odin bravely suffered in that strange, bright valley, before he was rewarded with a drink from that wonderful fountain; but we may be quite sure that never once was the good Allfather sorry for anything he had given up, or any suffering he had borne, for the sake of others.

TYR AND THE WOLF.

I.

Odin, the Allfather, sat one day on his high air-throne, and looking around him, far and wide, saw three fierce monsters. They were the children of the mischievous fire-god Loki, and Odin began to feel anxious, for they had grown so fast and were getting so strong that he feared they might do harm to the sacred city of Asgard. The wise father knew Loki had given strength to these dreadful creatures, and he saw that all this danger had come upon the Æsir from Loki's wickedness.

One of these monsters was a huge serpent, that Odin sent down into the ocean, where he grew so fast that his body was coiled around the whole world, and his tail grew into his own mouth. He was called the Midgard serpent.

The second monster was sent to Niflheim, the home of darkness, and shut up there.

The third, a fierce wolf, named Fenrir, was brought to Asgard, where Odin hoped he might be tamed by living among the Æsir, and seeing their good deeds, and hearing their kind words; but he grew more and more fierce, until only one of all the gods dared to feed him. This was the brave god, Tyr. He was a war-god, like Thor, and is sometimes called the Sword-god. Tyr was loved by all because he was so true and faithful.

Each day the dreadful wolf grew larger and stronger, till all at once, before the Æsir thought about it, he had become a very dangerous beast.

Father Odin always looked troubled when he saw Fenrir, the wolf, come to get his evening meal of meat from Tyr's hand, and at last one night, after the wolf had gone growling away to his lair, Odin called a meeting of the Æsir. He told them of his fears, saying they must find some plan for guarding themselves and their home against this monster. They could not slay him, for no one must ever be killed, and no blood must be shed, within the walls of the sacred city.

Thor was the first to speak: "Do not fear, Father Odin, for by to-morrow night we shall have Fenrir so safely bound that he cannot do us any harm. I will make a mighty chain, with the help of my hammer, Miölnir, and with it we will bind him fast!"

When the Æsir heard these words of Thor, they were glad, and all went home rejoicing—all save the Allfather, who was still troubled, for he well knew the danger, and feared that even the mighty Thor would find this task too much for him. But Thor seized his hammer, and strode off to his forge. There he worked the whole night long, and all through Asgard were heard the blows of Miölnir and the roaring of the bellows.

The next night, when the Æsir were gathered together, Thor brought forth his new-made chain, to test it. In came Fenrir, the wolf, and every one was surprised to see how willingly he let himself be bound with the chain. When Thor had riveted the last links together, the gods smiled, and began to praise him for his wonderful work; but all at once the wolf gave one bound forward, broke the great chain, and walked off to his lair as if nothing had happened.

Thor was much disappointed, still he did not lose courage. He said to the Æsir that he would make another chain, yet stronger. Again he set to work, and for three nights and three days the great Thor worked at his forge without resting.

While he worked his friends did not forget him. They came and looked on while he was busy, and, as they watched the mighty hammer falling with quick blows upon the metal, they talked to Thor or sang noble songs to cheer him; sometimes they brought him food and drink. One visitor, who was no friend, fierce Fenrir, the wolf, sometimes put his nose in at the door for a moment, and watched Thor at work; then, as he went away, Thor heard a strange sound like a wicked laugh.

At last the chain was finished, and Thor dragged it to the place of meeting. It was so heavy that even the mighty Thor could hardly lift it, or drag it as far as Odin's palace of Gladsheim. This time Fenrir was not so willing to be bound; but the gods coaxed him, and talked of his great strength, and told him they were sure he would easily break this chain also. After a while he agreed to let them put it around his neck.

This time Thor was sure the chain would hold firm, for never before had such a strong one been made. But soon, with a great shake and a fierce bound, the wolf broke away, and went off to his lair, snarling and showing his wicked teeth, while the broken chain lay on the ground.

Sadly the Æsir came together that night in Odin's palace, and this time Thor was not the first to speak; he sat apart and was silent.

First spoke Frey, the god of summer and king of the fairies. "Hearken to me, O lords of Asgard!"

THOR CHAINING FENRIR.

he said. "I have not won a brave name in battle, like the noble Tyr, neither have I done such mighty deeds as the great Thor and others of our heroes. Instead of fighting giants and monsters, I have spent most of my life in the woods, among the flowers, listening for hours to the birds. Many things have I watched, some perhaps that my brothers thought too small to be worthy of notice. I have learned many lessons, and the greatest of them all is to know how much power there is in little things, and to see how often the work, done quietly, and hidden from the eyes of men, is the finest and the most wonderful. Since we cannot make a chain strong enough to bind Fenrir, let us go to the little dwarfs, who work in silence and in darkness, and ask them to make us a chain!"

The Allfather's troubled face grew brighter as he heard Frey speak, and he bade him send a messenger quickly to the dwarfs, to order a chain made as soon as possible.

II.

So Frey went out, leaving the Æsir in their trouble, and came to his own lovely home, Alfheim. There everything was bright and peaceful, and the little elves were busy and happy. Frey found a trusty messenger, and sent him with all speed to the dwarfs underground, to order the new chain, and to return as soon as he could bring it. The faithful servant found the funny little dwarf workmen all busy in their dark rock chambers, far down inside the earth, while at one side, in a lighter place, sat their king. The messenger bowed before him, and told him his errand.

The dwarfs were a wicked race, but they were afraid of Odin, for they had not forgotten the talk he once had with them, when he sent them down to work in darkness underground, and since that time they never had dared disobey him. The dwarf king said it would take two days and two nights to make the chain, but it would be so strong that no one could break it.

While the busy dwarfs were at work, the messenger looked about at the many wonderful things: the great central fire which burns always in the middle of the earth, watched and fed with coal by the dwarfs; above this, the beds of coal, and bright precious diamonds, which the dwarfs took from the ashes of the fire. In another place he watched them putting gold and silver, tin and copper, into the cracks in the rocks, and he drank of the pure, underground water, which gives the Midgard people fresh springs.

After two days this messenger returned to the dwarf king. The king, holding out in his hand a fine, small chain, said to the messenger: "This may seem to you to be small and weak; but it is a most wonderful piece of work, for we have used in it all the strongest stuff we could find. It is made of six kinds of things: the noise made by the footfall of cats, the roots of stones, the beards of women, the voice of fishes, the spittle of birds, the sinews of bears. This chain can never be broken; and if you can once put it on Fenrir, he will never be able to throw it off."

Odin's messenger was glad to hear this, so he thanked the dwarf king, and promising him a large reward, he went on his way back to Asgard, where the Æsir were longing for his return, and were all rejoiced to see him with the magic chain.

Now Father Odin feared that Fenrir would not let them bind him a third time, so he proposed they should all take a holiday, and go out to a beautiful lake to the north of Asgard, where they would have games and trials of strength. The other gods were pleased with this plan, and all set out in Frey's wonderful ship, which was large enough to hold all the Æsir with their horses, and yet could be folded up small enough to go in one's pocket.

They landed on a lovely island in the lake, and after the races and games were over, Frey brought out the little chain, and asked them all to try to break it. Thor and Tyr tried in vain; then Thor said, "I do not believe any one but Fenrir can break it."

Now the wolf did not want to be bound again; but he was very proud of his strength, and, for fear of being called a coward, said at last he would let them do it, if he might hold the right hand of one of the Æsir in his mouth while they bound him, as a sign that the gods did not mean to play any tricks.

When the gods heard this, they looked at each other, and all but one of them drew back. Only the brave, good Tyr stepping forward, quietly put his hand into Fenrir's mouth. The other gods then put the chain around the beast, and fastened it to a great rock. The fierce creature gave a leap to free himself, but the more he struggled the tighter grew the chain. The Æsir gathered about him in joy to see this, but their hearts were filled with sorrow when they saw that their noble Tyr had lost his right hand; the dreadful wolf had shut his teeth together in his rage, when he found he could not get free.

Thus the brave Tyr dared to risk danger for the sake of saving others, and gave up even his right hand to gain peace and happiness for Asgard.

FREYJA'S NECKLACE.

"YES, I really must have some flowers to wear to the feast to-night," said Freyja to her husband, Odur.

Freyja was the goddess of love and beauty; she was the most beautiful of all the Æsir, and every one loved to look at her charming face, and to hear her sweet voice.

"I think you look quite beautiful enough as you are, without flowers," Odur replied, but Freyja was not satisfied; she thought she would go and find her brother Frey, the god of summer, for he would give her a garland of flowers. So she wandered forth from Asgard on her way to Frey's bright home in Alfheim, where he lived among his happy, busy little elves. As Freyja walked along she was thinking of the feast to be given that night in Asgard, and knowing that all the gods and goddesses would be there, she wished to look her very best.

On and on she wandered, not thinking how far she was getting away from home. Finally the light began to grow fainter and fainter, and Freyja found herself in a strange place. The sunlight had faded away, but there was still a little light that came from lanterns carried by funny little dwarfs, who were busily working. Some were digging gold and gems, others were cleaning off the dirt from the precious stones, and polishing them to make them bright, while four little fellows were seated in one corner, putting the sparkling stones together into a wonderful necklace.

"What can that beautiful thing be?" thought Freyja. "If only I had that, it would surely make me look more beautiful than any one else at the feast to-night!" And the more she thought about it, the more she longed to get it. "Oh, I really must have it!" she said to herself, and with these words she stepped nearer to the four little men. "For what price will you sell me your necklace?" she asked.

The dwarfs looked up from their work, and when they saw Freyja's lovely face and heard her sweet voice, said, "Oh, if you will only look kindly upon us, and be our friend, you may have the necklace!"

FREYJA IN THE CAVE OF THE DWARFS.

Then a mocking laugh echoed again and again through the dark cavern, seeming to say, "How foolish you are to wish for these bright diamonds; they will not make you happy!" But Freyja snatched the necklace and ran out of the cavern. It did not please her to hear the teasing laugh of the dwarfs, and she wanted to get away from them as soon as possible.

At last she was once more out in the open air; she tried to be free and happy again, but a strange feeling of dread came over her, as if something were going to happen. Soon she came to a still pool of water, and, putting on the necklace, she bent over to look at her picture in the clear water. How beautiful the diamonds were! and how they sparkled in the sunshine! She must hasten home to show them to Odur.

The fair goddess soon reached Asgard, and hurried to the palace to find her husband. But Odur was not there. Over and over again she searched through all the rooms in vain; he had gone, and although Freyja had her beautiful necklace, she cared little for it without her dear husband.

Soon it was time to go to the feast, but Freyja would not go without Odur. She sat down and wept bitter tears; she felt no joy now for having the necklace, and no sorrow because she could not feast with the Æsir

If only Odur would come back, all would be well again. "I will go to the end of the world to find him!" said Freyja, and she began to make ready for her journey. Her chariot, drawn by two cats, was soon ready; but before she could start, she must first ask Father Odin to allow her to go.

"Allfather, I beg you give me leave to go to look for my Odur in every corner of the world!"

The wise father replied, "Go, fair Freyja, and may you find whom you seek."

Then she started forth. First to the Midgard world the goddess of beauty went, but no one in all the world had seen or heard of Odur. Down under the earth, to Niflheim, and even to Utgard, the land of giants, she wandered, but still no one had seen or even heard of her husband. Poor Freyja wept many tears, and wherever the teardrops fell, and sank into the ground, they turned into glistening gold.

At last the sad goddess returned to her own palace alone. She still wore the wonderful necklace, which was called Brisingamen.

One night, when the hour was late, all the Æsir were asleep, except the ever watchful Heimdall, who heard soft footsteps, like those of a cat, near Freyja's palace. He listened, and thought, "That is surely some one bent on mischief; I must follow him."

When Heimdall reached the palace, he found it was Loki, changed into another form, creeping softly about. Heimdall quietly watched him, and saw him glide in to Freyja's bedside, where the fair goddess lay asleep, wearing her beautiful necklace. Loki had come to steal the necklace, but when he saw that she was lying on the clasp of the chain, so that he could not undo it without waking her, he changed himself into a gnat, and, crawling along on the pillow, stung her just enough to make her turn over, but not enough to wake her. Then he unclasped the chain and ran off with it as fast as he could.

But Heimdall was not going to let the thief get away. As soon as Loki found that he was followed, he took his other form, a little flame of fire; Heimdall then took *his* other shape, and became a shower of rain, to put out the fire; but Loki, quick and watchful, changed himself into a bear, to catch the rain. Then Heimdall too became a bear, and a fierce fight began. At last the rain-god conquered, and forced wicked Loki to give back the necklace to Freyja.

The whole land seemed to feel sorry for poor, lonely Freyja; the leaves fell from the trees, the bright flowers faded, and the singing birds flew away.

Once more the fair goddess went forth from Asgard to seek Odur. Away, away to the far-off sunny south she wandered, and there, where the myrtle trees and the oranges grow, at last she found her long-lost husband.

Then hand in hand the two turned northward again, to their home, and so happy were they together, that they spread joy and happiness around them as they passed along. Everywhere the ice and snow thawed before them, green grass and sweet flowers sprang up behind their footsteps, the birds sang their sweetest songs, the warm summer came back to the north lands, and every one was glad and joyful, for lovely, smiling Freyja was at home again.

"White were the moorlands
And frozen, before her;
Green were the moorlands
And blooming, behind her.
Out of her gold locks
  Shaking the spring flowers,
Out of her garments
Shaking the south wind,
Around in the birches
Awaking the throstles,
Beautiful Freyja came."

—KINGSLEY.

THE HAMMER OF THOR.

SIF was the wife of mighty Thor, the thunder-god, and she was very proud of her beautiful golden hair, which she combed and braided with great care. One morning when she awoke she was filled with grief and dismay to find that her lovely hair had been cut off in the night, while she slept. Her husband happened to be away that day, but when he came home late at night, Sif was careful to keep out of his sight, she felt so ashamed of her shorn head.

Thor, however, soon called for Sif, and when he saw what had been done to her, he was very angry. Now Thor had a quick temper; every one feared his fierce anger. "Who could have done this wicked deed?" thought he. "There is only one among all the Æsir who would think of doing such a thing!"

Thor lost no time in finding Loki, and that mischief-god had to admit that he was the guilty one, but he begged Thor to give him just a few days, and he promised to get something for Sif that would make her look more beautiful than ever. So Thor decided to give him a chance to try, and commanded him to give back to Sif her golden hair.

Now Loki knew a place where some wonderful workmen lived, so he went off, as fast as he could go, to Niflheim, the home of the dwarfs, under the earth, and asked one of them to make quickly some golden hair for Sif. Besides this, he asked for two gifts to carry to the gods Odin and Frey, so that they might be on his side if Thor should bring his complaint before the Æsir.

Loki did not have to wait long before the dwarf brought him a quantity of beautiful hair, spun from the finest golden thread. It had the wonderful power of growing just like real hair, as soon as it touched any one's head. Besides this, there was a spear for Odin, which never missed its aim, no matter how far it was thrown, and for Frey, a ship that could sail through the air as well as the sea. Although it was large enough to hold all the gods and their horses, yet it could be folded so that it was small enough to put in one's pocket.

Loki was greatly pleased with these wonderful presents, and declared that this dwarf must be the most skillful workman of them all. Now it happened that another dwarf, named Brock, heard him say this, and he told Loki that he was sure he and his brother could make more wonderful things than these.

Loki did not believe that could be done, but he told Brock to try his skill; the Æsir should judge between them and the one who should fail in the trial must lose his head.

Then Brock called his brother, Sindri, and they set to work at once. They first built a great fire, and Sindri threw into it a lump of gold; then he told Brock to blow the bellows while he went out, and be sure not to stop blowing until he should come back.

Brock thought this an easy task, but his brother had not long been gone when a huge fly came in and buzzed about his face, and bothered him so that he could hardly keep on blowing; still he was able to finish his work, so that when Sindri came back, they took out of the fire an enormous wild boar, which gave out light, and could travel through the air with wonderful speed.

On the second day Sindri threw another lump of gold into the fire, and left his brother to blow the bellows. Again the buzzing, stinging fly came, and was even more troublesome than before; but Brock tried very hard to be patient, and was able to bear it without stopping his work until Sindri returned.

Then they took from the fire a magic ring of gold, from which eight new rings fell off every week.

The third day a lump of iron was put into the fire, and Brock was again left alone. In came the cruel fly, — have you guessed that it was really that mischief-maker Loki? He bit the poor little dwarf so hard on the forehead that the blood ran down into his eyes, and blinded him so that he could no longer see to do his work.

Poor Brock had to stop just before Sindri came home, but not before the hammer which they were making in the fire was nearly finished, only the handle came out rather too short. This magic hammer was named Miölnir. It had the power of never missing its mark, and would always return to the hand which threw it.

When Loki appeared at last before the Æsir, with the two dwarf brothers and their gifts, it was declared that they had made the finest things, for the hammer, which was given to Thor, would surely be most useful in keeping the giants out of Ásgard.

When Loki found that the judgment was against him, he started to run away; but Thor soon made him turn back by threatening to throw his hammer after him.

Then Loki had to collect his wits, and think of some way to escape losing his head, instead of making the dwarfs pay the forfeit, as he had expected. At last he told Brock and Sindri that they could have his head, according to the agreement, but as nothing had been said about his neck, they could not, of course, touch that.

Thus the wily Loki, by his wit, saved his life.

THOR'S WONDERFUL JOURNEY.

I.

One morning Thor asked Loki, the fire-god, if he would like to go forth with him to Utgard, the stronghold of the giants, where he was going to try, with his mighty hammer, to conquer those fierce enemies of Asgard. Loki was glad to go with him, and the two gods started forth in Thor's chariot, drawn by two goats.

Thor often went on a journey, so the dwellers in Asgard did not wonder to see him getting ready for a long drive. As Thor and Loki drove along, the heavy chariot rattled, and made the thunder echo among the hills. People in our world, down below in Midgard, heard the rumbling, and said: "What a heavy thunderstorm! How the thunder crashes and rumbles!"

Toward evening the travelers stopped at a peasant's hut, and Thor, alighting from his chariot, went to the door of the house, to ask shelter for the night.

"I will gladly give you a room, but I have no food in the house," said the man who opened the door.

"Oh, never mind that," said Thor; "I will provide the food." So Thor and Loki stopped for the night at the peasant's hut. They found the family within, the man, his wife, and two children, a boy and a girl. All looked on in great surprise to see Thor kill his two goats and cook them for the evening meal. "Eat all you wish of the meat," said Thor, "but be careful not to break any of the bones; throw them all into the two skins which I have spread upon the floor."

Now the boy, whose name was Thialfe, wondered why Thor should say this, and as he happened to have a piece of the leg-bone, he thought there could be no harm in breaking it open, to get out the soft marrow to eat. Thor was just then talking to Loki, and did not notice what had been done; but next morning the boy learned a lesson that he never forgot.

When Thor was ready to start off again, next day, he held his magic hammer over the skins in which lay the bones. All at once the goats became whole again, and stood there just the same as before, except that one of them limped with his hind leg.

Then the young Thialfe knew why Thor had told them not to break the bones. At first, when he saw Thor's angry face, and how he grasped his hammer, the boy was frightened, and wanted to run away; but soon he remembered it would be cowardly to do that, so he went to Thor, and asked his forgiveness. Now the mighty thunder-god, though often angry, was always just and kind. After scolding the boy as he deserved, he freely forgave him, and said that he and his sister might go along with Loki and himself on their journey.

II.

The four started off, after saying good-by to the peasant and his wife, leaving in their charge the chariot and goats, for it seemed best to finish the journey on foot.

At nightfall they entered a thick forest, through which they wandered on for miles, when all at once they came upon a house, and a strange-looking house it was. The wide front door opened into a big room; at the left was a small room, and just opposite the front door were four long, narrow rooms.

The travelers wondered to find a house in the depths of a forest, but they were glad to have shelter for the night, and all lay down for a good rest. Soon after midnight they were awakened by groans

THOR AND LOKI IN THE CHARIOT.

and strange sounds, and the earth began to tremble. Thor sent his companions into the farthest room, grasped his hammer, and stood on guard by the door. At daybreak he started forth to find out what had caused the noise. He had not gone far when he came upon a huge giant, lying on the ground asleep, and Thor found that he was making the earth tremble with his snoring, which must have been the sound they had heard in the night.

While Thor was looking at the giant, he awoke, and spoke to the god. "Ho, ho! I think you little fellow must be Thor, of whom I have often heard, but really, I did not think you were quite so small! Now the sun is up, and I must be off; but where is my other glove? Oh, here it is, on the ground!" And the giant stooped and picked up his glove, which was the very house in which our four travelers had spent the night, with the big front door where the hand went in, the thumb for the one side-room, and the four narrow finger-rooms opposite the door.

"If you are going my way, you may come along with me," said the giant. So they journeyed together for one day, but even mighty Thor could hardly keep up with the giant's long strides.

When night came, the giant stopped under a large oak tree, and said, "I am going to sleep; you may eat your supper, if you wish; here is a bag full of things." Saying this, he fell asleep, and was soon snoring. But when Thor tried to open the bag of food, he could not untie the cord. This made him angry, for the giant had tied up their food with his own. He looked at the huge figure lying before him asleep, and when he thought what a mean trick the giant had played upon them, Thor seized the magic hammer, and threw it at him.

"Did a leaf fall on me?" said the giant, sleepily. "Haven't you eaten your supper yet? Well, I am going to sleep again." And soon he was snoring louder than before. Thor grasped his hammer tighter than ever, and threw it with such strength that it seemed as though it must surely have killed the giant; but again he rubbed his eyes, and said, "I thought an acorn fell on my head!" He had hardly spoken when he was asleep again.

Then a third time Thor hurled his hammer with all his strength, and it seemed to hit his enemy in the forehead, and was buried out of sight, but the giant only said: "I think there must be birds overhead in this tree; I thought a feather dropped down on me. Are you awake, Thor? I think we'd better be going on with our journey, and if you are bound to go to Utgard, I will show you the way, but I advise you to go home instead; you will find bigger fellows than I in Utgard!"

But Thor had made up his mind to go on, and nothing could make him change. At noontime the four friends left their giant guide, whose path led another way. They had not traveled far when Thor spied a large city looming up before them, and soon they came to Utgard, the home of the fierce giants.

Although it was surrounded by high walls, Thor and his friends were able to creep through the bars of the great gate. When they came to the palace and found its door open, they went in, and there sat all the giants with their king, Utgard-Loki, at their head. A quite different Loki was this giant king from the mischievous fire-god, the Loki from Asgard, who now stood before him.

III.

Upon seeing the four strangers, the king of the giants said: "Why, this must be the god Thor. I really did not suppose that you were such a little fellow, Thor! but probably you are stronger than you look. Now, before you sit down at our table, you must each show some proof of your strength!"

Then Loki, who was very hungry, said he was sure he could eat more than any one else; so the king called one of the giants to come forth, saying to Loki, "If you can indeed eat more than one of my men, you will perform a great feat."

A huge trough, full of meat, was brought in, and Loki began eating at one end, while the giant began at the other. They reached the center together; but Loki had eaten only the meat, while the giant had devoured meat, bones, trough, and all.

Thialfe, the peasant boy, took his turn next, and boasted that he was the fastest runner of them all. "Oh," said the king, "it will be a most wonderful feat if you can win a race against one of my men!" The first time Thialfe ran the course he kept ahead until near the end, and was beaten by only a few yards. The second time he came off worse, and the third time he was only halfway around when the giant had reached the goal.

Thor, however, was not at all cast down by the failure of the others, and he proposed to try a drinking match. So the king brought forth a long drinking horn, saying, "My men usually empty this in one draught, if they are very thirsty, though sometimes they have to take it in two swallows, or even three."

Then Thor put his lips to the drinking horn, and took one long, deep pull, thinking he had surely emptied it, but to his surprise, the water had lowered only a few inches. Again he lifted the horn, feeling sure he should empty it this time, yet he did no better than before. The king said, "You have left a great deal for your last drink!"

This made Thor try his very best; but it was of no use, he could not empty the horn.

"So you are not as strong as you seemed, after all! Do you care to try anything else?" said the king of the giants, in a mocking tone.

"Oh, certainly, anything you like!" replied Thor.

"Well," said the king, "I will give you something easy this time, since I see you are not as strong as I expected. You may try to lift this cat from the floor; it would be mere child's play for one of my men."

Thor put out his hand to lift the cat, but he could raise only one paw, though he used all his strength.

"Well, it is no more than I expected!" said the king; "you boast of your strength, but you do not show it to us."

By this time Thor was getting very angry, and he spoke fiercely, "I will challenge any one of you to fight with me!"

The king looked about the hall to find some one small enough to wrestle with Thor. Then he said, "All my men are too large, I shall have to send for one of the women!" Soon a bent old woman came hobbling in, and Thor thought it would be nothing to overcome her; but the longer they wrestled, the stronger the old woman became, and at last, when it was plain that she was going to win, and Thor had been thrown down upon the floor, the king called to them to stop.

Thor and his friends were then invited to sit down at the feast, and the next morning, after a good breakfast, they started on their journey homeward. Utgard-Loki, the giant king, went with them to the city gate, and when he was about to leave them, said, "Do you find it as easy as you expected to overthrow the giants?"

"No," said Thor, who was too honest to hide his shame, "I am vexed that I have done so little, and I know that after this failure, you will all laugh at my weakness."

"No, indeed," replied the king; "since you are now well outside our stronghold I will tell you the truth about what you saw there, and I will take good care not to let you get in again. You have greatly surprised us all, for we did not dream that you were so strong, and I have had to use magic to hold out against you.

"When you met the first giant in the forest you would have killed him with your hammer, if he had not put a mountain between himself and you. Loki was a wonderful eater, but we matched him against fire, and who can devour more than fire? The boy was a swift runner, and I had to make him race against thought, in order to beat him; what can be swifter than thought? The horn, from which you drank, was the ocean, and you took such a mighty draught, that the people in Midgard saw the tide ebb. It was really not a cat you tried to lift, but the Midgard Serpent, and you pulled him so far that we feared he would let go his hold. Then you wrestled with Old Age, and who is there that can overcome Old Age?"

With these words the giant king vanished, and Thor, upon looking around, saw the city of Utgard was also gone.

Then silently, but with many thoughts of these strange things, Thor and Loki, with the boy and the girl, made their way back to Asgard.

HOW THOR LOST HIS HAMMER.

"COME, Loki, are you ready? My goats are eager to be off!" cried Thor, as he sprang into his chariot, and away they went, thundering over the hills. All day long they journeyed, and at night they lay down to rest by the side of a brook.

When Baldur, the bright sun-god, awoke them in the morning, the first thing Thor did was to reach out for Miölnir, his magic hammer, which he had carefully laid by his side the night before.

"Why, Loki!" cried he. "Alas, my hammer is gone! Those evil frost giants must have stolen it from me while I slept. How shall we hold Asgard against them without my hammer? They will surely take our stronghold!"

"We must go quickly and find it!" replied Loki. "Let us ask Freyja to lend us her falcon garment."

Now the goddess, Freyja, had a wonderful garment made of falcon feathers, and whoever wore it looked just like a bird. As you may suppose, this was sometimes a very useful thing. So Thor and Loki went quickly back to Asgard, and drove with all speed to Freyja's palace, where they found her sitting among her maidens. "Asgard is in great danger!" said Thor, "and we have come to you, fair goddess, to ask if you will lend us your falcon garment, for my hammer has been carried off, and we must go in search of it."

"Surely," answered Freyja, "I would lend you my falcon cloak, even if it were made of gold and silver!"

Then Loki quickly dressed himself in Freyja's garment and flew away to the land of the frost giants, where he found their king making collars of gold for his dogs, and combing his horses. As Loki came near, he looked up and said, "Ah, Loki, how fare the mighty gods in Asgard?"

"The Æsir are in great trouble," replied Loki, "and I am sent to fetch the hammer of Thor."

"And do you think I am going to be foolish enough to give it back to you, after I have had all the trouble of getting it into my power?" said the king. "I have buried it deep, deep, down in the earth, and there is only one way by which you can get it again. You must bring me the goddess Freyja to be my wife!"

Loki did not know what to say to this, for he felt sure that Freyja would never be willing to go away from Asgard to live among the fierce giants; but as he saw no chance of getting the hammer, he flew back to Asgard, to see what could be done.

Thor was anxiously looking out for him. "What news do you bring, Loki?" cried he. "Have you brought me my hammer again?"

"Alas, no!" said Loki. "I bring only a message from the giant king. He will not give up your hammer until you persuade Freyja to marry him!"

Then Thor and Loki went together to Freyja's palace, and the fair goddess greeted them kindly, but when she heard their errand, and found they wished her to marry the cruel giant, she was very angry, and said to Thor, "You should not have been so careless as to lose your hammer; it is all your own fault that it is gone, and I will never marry the giant to help you get it again."

Thor then went to tell Father Odin, who called a meeting of all the Æsir, for it was a very serious matter they were to consider. If the king of the giants only knew the power of the mighty hammer, he might storm Asgard, and carry off the fair Freyja to be his bride.

THOR'S BATTLE WITH THE FROST GIANTS.

So the Æsir met together in their great judgment hall, in the palace of Gladsheim; long and anxiously they talked over their peril, trying to find some plan for saving Asgard from these enemies. At last Heimdall, the faithful watchman of the rainbow bridge, proposed a plan.

"Let us dress Thor," said he, "in Freyja's robes, braid his hair, and let him wear Freyja's wonderful necklace, and a bridal veil!"

"No, indeed!" cried Thor, angrily, "you would all laugh at me in a woman's dress; I will do no such thing! We must find some other way." But when no other way could be found, at last Thor was persuaded to try Heimdall's plan, and the Æsir went to work to dress the mighty thunder-god like a bride. He was the tallest of them all, and, of course, he looked very queer to them in his woman's clothes, but he would be small enough beside a giant. Then they dressed Loki to look like the bride's waiting-maid, and the two set off for Utgard, the stronghold of the giants.

When the giant king saw them coming he bade his servants make ready the wedding feast, and invited all his giant subjects to come and celebrate his marriage with the lovely goddess Freyja.

So the wedding party sat down to the feast, and Thor, who was always a good eater, ate one ox and eight salmon, and drank three casks of mead. The king watched him, greatly surprised to see a woman eat so much, and said: —

> "Where hast thou seen
> Such a hungry bride!"

But the watchful Loki, who stood near by, as the bride's waiting-maid, whispered in the king's ear, "Eight nights has Freyja fasted and would take no food, so anxious was she to be your bride!"

This pleased the giant, and he went toward Thor, saying he must kiss his fair bride. But when he lifted the bridal veil, such a gleam of light shot from Thor's eyes that the king started back, and asked why Freyja's eyes were so sharp.

Again Loki replied, "For eight nights the fair Freyja has not slept, so greatly did she long to reach here!" This again pleased the king, and he said, "Now let the hammer be brought and given to the bride, for the hour has come for our marriage!"

All this time Thor was so eager to get his treasure back that he could hardly keep still, and if it had not been for what the wily Loki said, he might have been found out too soon. But at last the precious hammer was brought and handed to the bride, as was always the custom at weddings; as soon as Thor grasped it in his hand, he threw off his woman's robes and stood out before the astonished giants.

Then did the mighty Thunderer sweep down his foes, and many of the cruel frost giants were slain. Once more the sacred city of Asgard was saved from danger, for Thor was its defender, and he was careful never again to let his magic hammer be taken from him.

Besides the hammer, Thor had two other precious things, his belt of strength, which doubled his power when he tightened it, and his iron glove, which he put on when he was going to throw the hammer.

"I am the God Thor,
I am the War God,
I am the Thunderer!
Here in my Northland,
My fastness and fortress,
Reign I forever!

"Here amid icebergs
Rule I the nations;
This is my hammer,
Miölnir the mighty;
Giants and sorcerers
Cannot withstand it!

"These are the gauntlets
Wherewith I wield it,
And hurl it afar off;
This is my girdle,
Whenever I brace it
Strength is redoubled!"

— LONGFELLOW

A GIFT FROM FRIGGA.

LONG years ago there lived a peasant and his wife, who led a quiet, busy life on their little farm at the foot of a mountain. While the wife was busy indoors with her housework, her husband watched his flocks in the fields, or sometimes wandered up the mountain-side to hunt for game, which he would carry home for dinner.

One day he had strayed farther than usual, and found himself on the top of the mountain, where the ground was covered with ice and snow. All at once he came upon a high arched doorway opening into a great glacier, and he passed through to see whither it might lead.

The passageway widened out into a wonderful cavern, like a broad hall, sparkling with precious stones, and long, shining stalactites, that looked like icicles of marble. In the midst stood a beautiful goddess, surrounded by fair maidens, all dressed in silvery robes, and crowned with flowers.

The shepherd was so overcome by the wonder of this sight that he sank upon his knees. Then the goddess stretched forth her hands and gave him her blessing, telling him to choose whatever he wished, to carry home from the cavern. The man was no longer afraid when he heard her kind voice speaking to him, so he looked about, and at last humbly asked to have the pretty blue flowers which the fair one held in her hand.

The lovely goddess Frigga, or Holda, as the German people called her, smiled kindly, and told the poor shepherd he had made a wise choice. She gave him her bunch of blue flowers, with a measure of seed, saying to him, "You will live and be prosperous so long as the flowers do not fade."

The peasant bowed thankfully before the goddess, and when he rose she had vanished, and he was alone on the mountain-side, just as usual, with no cavern, no sparkling stones, and no fair maidens to be seen. If it had not been for the pretty blue flowers and the measure of seed in his hand, he would have thought it all a dream.

He hurried homeward to tell his wife, who was angry when she heard the story, for she thought he had made such a foolish choice. "How much better it would have been," said she, "if you had brought home some of those precious stones you tell about, which are worth money, instead of these good-for-nothing flowers!"

The poor man bore her angry words quietly, and made the best of what he had. He went to work at once to sow his seeds, which he found, to his surprise, were enough to plant several fields.

Every morning before he led his flock to pasture, and on his way home at night, he watched the little green shoots growing in his fields. Even his wife was pleased when she saw the lovely blue blossoms of the flax opening; then, after they had withered and fallen, the seeds formed. Sometimes it seemed to the good man, as he stood in the twilight looking over his field, that he saw a misty form, like the beautiful goddess, stretching out her hands over the field of flax, to give it her blessing.

When at length the seeds had ripened, Frigga came again to show the peasant how to gather his harvest of flax, and to teach his wife to spin and weave it into fine linen, which she bleached in the sun. The people came from far and near to buy the linen, and the peasant and his wife found themselves busy and happy, with money enough and to spare.

When they had lived many years, and were growing old among their children and grandchildren, the peasant noticed one day that the bunch of blue flowers, given to him so many years before, and which had always kept bright, were beginning to fade; then he knew he had not much longer to stay.

He climbed slowly up the mountain-side, and found the door of the cavern open. A second time he went in, and the kind goddess Frigga took the peasant by the hand, and led him away to stay with her, where she always took care of him.

Frigga was the queen of the gods, and she helped her husband, Odin, govern the world. It was her part to look after the children, and help the mothers take care of their families.

THE STEALING OF IDUNA

I.

ODIN, the wise father of the gods, started off one day on a journey through Midgard, the world of men, to see how his people were getting on, and to give them help. He took with him his brother Hönir, the light-giver, and Loki, the fire-god. Loki, you know, was always ready to go wherever he could have any fun or do any mischief.

All the morning they went about among the homes of Midgard, and whenever Odin found busy, faithful workers, he was sure to leave behind some little thing which would hardly be noticed, a straw in the farmer's barn, or a kernel of grain in the furrow by the plow, or a bit of iron at the blacksmith's forge; but always happiness and plenty followed his little gift.

At noontime Loki was so hungry that he begged Odin to stop for dinner; so when they came to a shady spot by the bank of a river, the three gods chose it for their resting-place.

Odin threw himself down under a tree and began to read his little book of runes, or wise sayings, but Loki began to make a fire and get ready for the feast. Then he started off to a farmhouse near by, leaving Hönir to cook the meat which they had brought.

As Loki came near the farmhouse, he thought to himself, "I will change myself into a cat, and then I can have a better chance to spy about." So he changed himself into a black cat, and jumping upon the kitchen window-sill, he saw the farmer's wife taking some cakes out of the oven. They smelled so good and looked so tempting that Loki said to himself, "What a prize those cakes would be for our dinner!"

Just then the woman turned back to the oven to get more cakes, and Loki snatched those which she had laid on the table. The good housewife soon missed her cakes; she looked all about, and could not think what had become of them, but just as she was taking the last lot from the oven, she turned quickly around, and saw the tail of a cat whisking out of the window.

"There!" cried she, "that wicked black cat has stolen my nice cakes. I will go after him with my broom!" But by the time she reached the door all she could see was a cow walking in her garden, and when she came there to drive her away, nothing was to be seen except a big raven and six little ones flying overhead.

Then the mischievous Loki went back to the river bank, where he had left his two friends, and showed them the six cakes, boasting of the good joke he had played upon the poor woman. But Odin did not think it was a joke. He scolded Loki for stealing, and said, "It is a shame for one of the Æsir to be a thief! Go back to the farmhouse, and put these three black stones on the kitchen table."

Loki knew that the stones meant something good for the poor woman, and he did not wish to go back to the house; but he had to do as the Allfather told him. As he went along he heard his friends the foxes, who put their heads out of their holes and laughed at his tricks, for the foxes thought Loki was the biggest thief of them all.

Changing himself into an owl, Loki flew in at the kitchen window, and dropped from his beak the three stones, which, when they fell upon the white table, seemed to be three black stains.

The next time the good woman came into her kitchen, she was surprised to find that the dinner was all cooked. And so the wonderful stones that Odin had sent brought good luck; the housewife always found her food ready cooked, and all her jars and boxes filled with good things to eat, and never again was in need. The other women all said she was the best housekeeper in the village, but one thing always troubled her, and that was the table with the three black stains. She scrubbed, and scrubbed, but could never make it white again.

And now we must go back to Loki. He was very hungry by this time, and hoped that Hönir would have the meat nicely cooked when he came back to the river bank, but when they took it out of the kettle, they found it was not cooked at all. So Odin went on reading his book of runes, not thinking about food, while Hönir and Loki watched the fire, and at the end of an hour they looked again at the meat.

"Now, it will surely be done this time!" said Loki, but again they were disappointed, for the meat in the kettle was still raw. Then they began to look about to see what magic might be at work, and at last spied a big eagle sitting on a tree near the fire. All at once the bird spoke, and said, "If you will promise to give me all the meat I can eat, it shall be cooked in a few minutes."

The three friends agreed to this, and in a short time, as the bird had promised, the meat was well done. Loki was so hungry he could hardly wait to get it out of the kettle, but suddenly the eagle pounced down upon it, and seized more than half, which made Loki so angry that he took up a stick to beat the bird, and what do you think happened? Why, the stick, as soon as it touched the bird's back, stuck fast there, and Loki found he could not let go his end of it. Then away flew the eagle, carrying Loki with him, over the fields and over the tree-tops, until it seemed as though his arms would be torn from his body. He begged for mercy, but the bird flew on and on. At last Loki said, "I will give you anything you ask, if you will only let me go!"

Now the eagle was really the cruel storm giant Thiassi, and he said, "I will never let you go until you promise to get for me, from Asgard, the lovely goddess Iduna, and her precious apples!"

When Odin and Hönir saw Loki whisked off through the air, they knew that the eagle must be one of their giant enemies, so they hurried home to Asgard to defend their sacred city. Just as they came to Bifröst, the rainbow bridge, Loki joined them; but he took care not to tell them how the eagle came to let him go.

Odin felt sure that Loki had been doing something wrong, but knowing very well that Loki would not tell him the truth, he made up his mind not to ask any questions.

II.

The goddess Iduna, whom Loki was to tempt away out of Asgard, was the dearest of them all. She was the fair goddess of spring and of youth, and all the Æsir loved her. Her garden was the loveliest spot, with all sorts of bright, sweet flowers, birds singing by day and night, little chattering brooks under the great trees, and everything happy and fresh. The gods loved to go and sit with Iduna, and rest in her beautiful garden, within the walls of Asgard.

There was another delightful thing in the garden, and that was Iduna's casket. This was a magic box filled with big, golden-red apples, which she always gave her friends to taste. These wonderful apples were not only delicious to eat, but whoever tasted them, no matter how tired or feeble he might be, would feel young and strong again. So the dwellers in Asgard ate often of this wonderful fruit, which kept them fresh and young, fit to help the people in the world of Midgard. The casket in which Iduna kept her apples was always filled, for whenever she took out one, another came in its place; but no one knew where it came from, and only the goddess of youth, herself, could take the apples from the box, for if any one else tried, the fruit grew smaller and smaller, as the hand came nearer, until at last it vanished away.

A few days after Loki's bargain with the giant Thiassi, Iduna was in her bright garden one morning, watering the flowers, when her husband, Bragi, came to say good-by to her, because he must go on a journey.

Loki watched him start off, and thought, "Now, here is my chance to tempt Iduna away from Asgard." After a while he went to the garden, and found the lovely goddess sitting among her flowers and birds. She looked up at Loki with such a sweet smile, as he came near, that he felt almost ashamed of his cruel plan; but he sat down on a grassy bank, and asked Iduna for one of her magic apples.

After tasting it, he smacked his lips, saying, "Do you know, fair Iduna, as I was coming home toward Asgard one day, I saw a tree full of apples which were really larger and more beautiful than yours; I do wish you would go with me and see them."

"Why, how can that be?" said Iduna, "for Father Odin has often told me that my apples were the largest and finest he ever saw. I should so like to see those others, and I think I will go with you now, to compare them with mine."

"Come on, then!" said Loki; "and you'd better take along your own apples, so that we can try them with the others."

Now Bragi had often told Iduna that she must

IDUNA GIVING LOKI THE APPLE.

never wander away from home, but, thinking it would do no harm to go such a little way, just this once, she took the casket of apples in her hand and went with Loki. They had hardly passed through the garden gate, when she began to wish herself back again, but Loki, taking her by the hand, hurried along to the rainbow bridge.

They had no sooner crossed over Bifröst than Iduna saw a big eagle flying toward them. Nearer and nearer he came, until at last he swooped down and seized poor Iduna with his sharp talons, and flew away with her to his cold, barren home. There she stayed shut up for many long dreary months, always longing to get back to Asgard, to see Bragi and her lovely garden.

The giant Thiassi had long been planning that if he could only once get the fair goddess of youth in his power, he would eat her magic apples, and so get strength enough to conquer the Æsir; but now, after all, she would not give him even one of them, and when he put his hand into the casket, the apples grew smaller and smaller, until at last they vanished, so that he could not get even a taste.

This cruel storm giant kept poor Iduna closely shut up in a little rock chamber, hoping that some day he could force her to give him what he wanted. All day long she heard the sea beating on the rocks below her gloomy cell, but she could not look out, for the only window was a narrow opening in the rock, high up above her head. She saw no one but the giant, and his serving-women, who waited upon her.

When these women first came to her, Iduna was surprised to see that they were not ugly or stern-looking, and, when she looked at their fair, smiling faces, she hoped they would be friendly and pitiful to her in her trouble. She begged them to help her, and, with many tears, told them her sad story; but still they kept on smiling, and when they turned their backs, Iduna saw that they were hollow. These were the Ellewomen, who had no hearts, and so could never be sorry for any one. When one is in trouble, it is very hard to be with Ellewomen.

Every day the giant came to ask Iduna, in his terrible voice, if she had made up her mind to give him the apples. Iduna was frightened, but she always had courage enough to say "No," for she knew it would be false and cowardly to give to a wicked giant these precious gifts which were meant for the high gods. Although it was hard to be a prisoner, and to see no one but the cold, fair Ellewomen who kept on smiling at her tears, she knew it was far better to belong to the bright Æsir, even in prison, than to be a giant, or an Ellewoman, no matter how free or smiling they might be.

III.

All this while the dwellers in Asgard were sad and lonely without their dear Iduna. At first they went to her garden, as before, but they missed the bright goddess, and soon the garden itself grew dreary. The fresh green leaves turned brown and fell, the flowers faded, no new buds opened. No bird-songs were heard, and the saddest thing of all was that now the gods had no more of the wonderful apples to keep them fresh and strong, while two strangers, named Age and Pain, walked about the city of Asgard, and the Æsir felt themselves growing tired and feeble.

Every day they watched for Iduna's return; at last, when day after day had passed, and still she did not come, a meeting of all the gods and goddesses was called to talk over what they should do, and where they should search for their lost sister.

Loki, you may be sure, took care not to show himself at the meeting; but when it was found out that Iduna had last been seen walking with him, Bragi went after him, and brought him in before all the Æsir.

Then Father Odin, who sat on his high throne, looking very tired and sad, said: "Oh, Loki, what is this that you have done? You have broken your promise of brotherhood, and brought sorrow upon Asgard! Fail not to bring home again our sister, or else come not yourself within our gates!"

Loki knew well that this command must be obeyed, and besides, even he was beginning to wish for Iduna again; so, borrowing the cloak of falcon feathers which belonged to the goddess Freyja, he put it on and set out for Utgard and the castle of the giant Thiassi, which was a gloomy cave in a high rock by the sea, and there he found poor Iduna shut up in prison.

By good luck, the giant was away fishing when Loki arrived, so he was able to fly in, without being seen, through the narrow opening in Iduna's rock cell. You would have taken him to be just a falcon bird, but Iduna knew it was really Loki, and was filled with joy to see him. Without stopping to talk, Loki quickly changed her into a nut, which he held fast in his falcon claws, and flew swiftly northward, over the sea, toward Asgard. He had not gone far when he heard a rushing noise behind them, and he knew it must be the eagle. Faster and faster flew the falcon with his precious nut; but the fierce eagle flew still faster after them.

Meanwhile, for five days, the dwellers in Asgard gathered together on the city walls, gazing southward, to watch for the coming of the birds, while Loki and Iduna, chased by Thiassi, the eagle, flew over the wide sea separating Utgard, the land of the giants, from Asgard. Each night the eagle was nearer his prey, and the watchers in the city were filled with fear lest he should overtake their friends.

At last they thought of a plan to help Iduna: gathering a great pile of wood by the city walls, they set fire to it. When Loki reached the place he flew safely through the thick smoke and flame, for you know he was the god of fire, and dropped down into the city with his little nut held fast in his falcon claws. But when the heavy eagle came rushing on after them, he could not rise above the heat of the fire, and, smothered by the smoke, fell down and was burned to death.

There was great joy in Asgard at having the dear Iduna back again; her friends gathered around her, and she invited them all into her garden, where the withered trees and flowers began to sprout and blossom; the gay birds came back, singing and building their nests, and the happy little brooks went dancing under the trees.

Iduna sat with Bragi among her friends, and they all feasted upon her golden apples; she was so thankful to be free, and at home in her garden again. Once more the Æsir became young and strong, and the two dark strangers went away, for happiness and peace had come back to Asgard.

SKADI.

WHILE Iduna's friends were still crowding about her, all joyful and glad at getting her home again, they spied some one afar off, coming toward Asgard.

As the figure drew nearer, they saw it was Skadi, the tall daughter of the frost giant Thiassi, who had chased Iduna; she was dressed all in white fur, and carried a shining hunting-spear and arrows. Slung over her shoulder were snowshoes and skates, for Skadi had come from her mountain home in the icy north. Very angry about the loss of her father, she had come to ask the Æsir why they had been so cruel to him.

Father Odin spoke kindly to her, saying, "We will do honor to your father by putting his eyes in the sky, where they will always shine as two bright stars, and the people in Midgard will remember Thiassi whenever they look up at night and see the two twinkling lights. Besides this, we will also give you gold and silver." But Skadi, thinking money could never repay her for the loss of her father, was still angry.

Loki looked at her stern face, and he said to himself, "If we can only make Skadi laugh, she will be more ready to agree to the plan," and he began to think of some way to amuse her. Taking a long cord he tied it to a goat; it was an invisible cord, which no one could see, and Loki himself held the other end of it. Then he began to dance and caper about, and the goat had to do just what Loki did. It really was such a funny sight, that all the gods shouted with laughter, and even poor, sorrowful Skadi had to smile.

When the Æsir saw this, they proposed another plan: Skadi might choose one of the gods for her husband, but she must choose, from seeing only his bare feet. The giantess looked at them all, as they stood before her, and when she saw the bright face of Baldur, more beautiful than all the rest, she agreed to their plan, saying to herself, "It might be that I should choose him, and then I should surely be happy."

The gods then stood in a row behind a curtain, so that Skadi could see nothing but their bare feet.

She looked carefully at them all, and at last chose the pair of feet which seemed to her the whitest, and of the finest shape, thinking those must be Baldur's; but when the curtain was taken away, she was surprised and sorry to find she had chosen Niörd, the god of the seashore.

The wedding took place at Asgard, and when the feasting was over, Skadi and Niörd went to dwell in his home by the sea. At first they were very happy, for Niörd was kind to his giant bride; but how could you expect one of the Æsir to live happily very long with a frost giantess for his wife?

Skadi did not like the roar of the waves, and hated the cries of the sea-gulls and the murmur of gentle summer winds. She longed for her frozen home, far away in the north, amid ice and snow.

And so they finally agreed that, for nine months of the year, Niörd should live with Skadi among her snowy mountains, where she found happiness in hunting over the white hills and valleys on her snowshoes, with her hunting dogs at her side, or skating on the ice-bound rivers and lakes. Then for the three short months of summer Skadi must live with Niörd in his palace by the sea, while he calmed the stormy ocean waves, and helped the busy fishermen to have good sailing for their boats.

Niörd loved to wander along the shore, his jacket

SKADI HUNTING IN THE MOUNTAINS.

trimmed with a fringe of lovely seaweeds and his belt made of the prettiest shells on the beach, with the friendly little sandpipers running before him, and beautiful gulls and other sea birds sailing in the air above his head. Sometimes he loved to sit on the rocks by the shore, watching the seals play in the sunshine, or feeding the beautiful swans, his favorite birds.

There is a kind of sponge, which the people in the north still call Niörd's glove, in memory of this old Norse god.

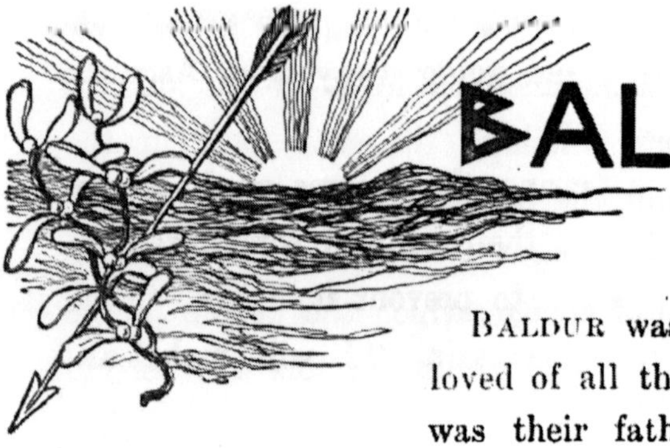

BALDUR.

I.

Baldur was the best beloved of all the gods. Odin was their father and king; to him they turned for help and wise advice, but it was to Baldur they went for loving words and bright smiles. The sight of his kind face was a joy to the Æsir, and to all the people of Midgard. They sometimes called him the god of light, a good name for him, because he truly gave to the world light and strength.

Baldur was the son of Odin and Frigga; he was the most gentle and lovely of all the gods. His beautiful palace in Asgard was bright and spotless; no evil creature could enter there; no one who had wrong thoughts could stay in that palace of love and truth.

At last, after the bright summer was over, for many days Baldur had looked sad and troubled. Some of the Æsir saw it, but most of all, his loving, watchful mother, Frigga. Baldur could not bear to worry his mother, so he kept his sorrow to himself, saying nothing about it; but at last Frigga drew his secret from him, and then his friends knew that Baldur had had dreams which told of coming trouble, dreams of his leaving all his friends and going away from Asgard, to dwell in another land.

Odin and Frigga, fearing the dreams might come true and they must lose their beloved son, began to think what they could do to prevent it.

Then the loving mother said, "I will make all things in the world promise not to hurt our son." And so Queen Frigga sent out for everything in the whole world, and everything came trooping to Asgard, to her palace. All living creatures came from the land, from the water, and from the air. All plants and trees came; all rocks, stones, and even the metals under the earth, where the busy dwarfs worked. Fire came, and water, as well as all poisons, and sickness. Everything promised not to harm the good Baldur, except one little plant called mistletoe, which was so small that Frigga did not send for it, feeling sure it could not do any harm.

"Now I am happy once more," said the queen, "for our Baldur is safe!" And she sat at peace in her beautiful palace, rejoicing that her dear son was free from all danger.

But Odin, the wise Allfather, still felt uneasy, even

after all these promises, fearing what might happen. So he took his eight-footed steed, Sleipnir, and rode forth from Asgard to the underworld to find Hela, the wise woman who ruled over that far-off land. She could tell everything that was going to happen, and she knew the names of all those who were coming to dwell with her. Odin was the only one wise enough to speak with Hela, for no one else knew the words that would call her forth from her dwelling; but when Odin called, she came to answer.

"Tell me," said he, "for whom are you making ready this costly room?"

"We make ready for Baldur, the god of light," replied Hela.

"Who, then, will slay Baldur, and bring such darkness and sorrow to Asgard?"

Again said the wise woman, "It is Hodur, Baldur's twin brother, who will slay the sun-god." And with these words she vanished.

Sadly Father Odin returned to Asgard, and told his wife the words of Hela; but Frigga was not troubled in her heart, for she felt sure that nothing would hurt her dear son.

II.

One beautiful sunny day at the end of summer the gods had all gone out to an open field beyond

Asgard to have some sports. As they all knew that nothing could hurt Baldur, they placed him at the end of the field for a target, and then took turns throwing their darts at him, just for the fun of seeing them fall off without hurting him. They thought this was showing great honor to Baldur, and he was pleased to join in the sport.

Loki happened to be away when they began to play, and when he came was angry in his heart that nothing could hurt Baldur.

"Why should he be so favored? I hate him!" said Loki to himself, and began at once to plan some evil.

All this while Queen Frigga sat in her palace, thinking of all her dear sons, and of how much good they did to men. As she sat thus, thinking, and spinning with her hands, there came a knock at the door. The queen called, "Come in!" and an old woman stood before her.

Frigga spoke kindly to her, and soon the old woman said she had passed by the field where the gods were playing, and throwing sharp weapons at Baldur.

"Oh, yes," said Frigga; "neither metal nor wood can hurt him, for all things in the world have given me their promise."

"What!" said the old woman; "do you mean that all things have really vowed to spare Baldur?"

"All," replied the queen, "except one little plant that grows on the eastern side of Asgard; it is called mistletoe, and I thought it too small and soft to do any harm."

Before long the old woman went away, and when she was quite out of sight of Frigga's palace, threw off her woman's clothes, and who do you suppose it was? Why, no woman at all, but that wicked Loki, of course, who hurried away out of Asgard, to find the poor little plant that did not know about Baldur's danger. When he came to the place where the plant grew, Loki cutting off a branch, quickly made a sharp arrow, which he carried back to the playground, where the Æsir were still at their game, all but one, Hodur, the god of darkness, Baldur's blind twin brother.

Then Loki went up to Hodur, and said to him in a low voice, "Why do you not join with the others in doing honor to Baldur?"

"I cannot see to take aim, you know, and besides, I have no weapon," said Hodur.

"Come, then, here is a fine new dart for you, and I will guide your hand," whispered wicked Loki; then he slipped the arrow of mistletoe wood into Hodur's hand and aimed it himself at Baldur, who stood there so bright and smiling.

Then poor blind Hodur heard a dreadful cry from all the gods: Baldur the Beautiful had fallen, struck by the arrow; he would now be taken away from them, to live with Hela in the underworld.

Every heart was filled with sorrow for this dreadful loss; but no one tried to punish him who had done the wicked deed, for they stood upon sacred ground, and the field was named the Peace-stead, or Place of Peace, where no one might hurt another. Besides, the gods did not know it was the false Loki who hated Baldur, that had struck him down.

When Frigga heard the sad news, she asked who would win her love by going to the underworld and begging Hela to let Baldur come back to them.

Hermod, the swift messenger-god, ready to do his mother's bidding, set forth at once on the long journey. Nine days and nights he traveled without resting, until he came to Hela's underworld. There he found Baldur, who was glad to see him, and sent messages to his friends in Asgard. Hela said Baldur might return to them on one condition: that every living creature, and everything in the world must weep for him.

So Hermod hastened back to Asgard, and when the Æsir heard Hela's answer, they sent out messengers over the world to bid all things weep for Baldur, their bright sun-god. Then did the beasts, the birds, the fishes, the flowers and trees, even stones and metals weep; as indeed we can see the teardrops come to all things when they are changed from heat to cold.

As the messengers were coming back to Asgard they met an old woman, whom they bade weep, but she replied, "Let Hela keep Baldur down below; why should I care?" When the Æsir heard of this, they thought it must have been the same old woman who went before to Frigga's palace, and we know who that was.

And so Baldur the beautiful, Baldur the bright, did not come back, and all the dwellers in Asgard were sad and sorrowful without him.

ÆGIR'S FEAST.

I.

ÆGIR was the ruler of the ocean, and his home was deep down below the tossing waves, where the water is calm and still. There was his beautiful palace, in the wonderful coral caves; its walls all hung with bright-colored seaweeds, and the floor of white, sparkling coral sand. Such wonderful sea-plants grew all about, and still more wonderful creatures, some, which you could not tell from flowers, waving their pretty fringes in the water; some sitting fastened to the rocks and catching their food without moving, like the sponges; others darting about and chasing each other.

"Deep in the wave is a coral grove,
Where the purple mullet and goldfish rove;
Where the sea-flower spreads its leaves of blue,
That never are wet with falling dew,

But in bright and changeful beauty shine
Far down in the green and glassy brine.
The floor is of sand, like the mountain drift,
And the pearl-shells spangle the flinty snow;
From coral rocks the sea-plants lift
Their boughs where the tides and billows flow.
The water is calm and still below,
For the winds and waves are absent there,
And the sands are bright as the stars that glow
In the motionless fields of upper air."
— PERCIVAL.

In that ocean home lived the lovely mermaids, who sometimes came up above the waves to sit on the rocks and comb their long golden hair in the sunshine. They had heads and bodies like beautiful maidens, with fish-tails instead of feet.

One day the gods in Asgard gave a feast, and Ægir was invited. He could not often leave home to visit Asgard, for he was always very busy with the ocean winds and tides and storms; but calling his daughters, the waves, he bade them keep the ocean quiet while he was away, and look after the ships at sea.

Then Ægir went over Bifröst, the rainbow bridge, to Asgard, where they had such a gay party and such feasting that he was sorry when the time came to go home; but at last he said good-by to Father Odin and the rest of the Æsir. He thanked them all for the pleasure they had given him, saying, "If only I had a kettle that held enough mead for us all to drink, I would invite you to visit me."

Thor, who was always glad to hear about eating and drinking, said, "I know of a kettle a mile wide and a mile deep; I will fetch it for you!"

Then Ægir was pleased, and set a day for them all to come to his great feast.

So Thor took with him his brother, the brave Tyr, who knew best how to find the kettle; and together they started off in Thor's thunder chariot, drawn by goats, on their way to Utgard, the home of the giants.

When they reached that land of ice and snow, they soon found the house of Hymir, the giant who owned "Mile-deep," as the big kettle was called. The gods were glad to find that the giant was not at home, and his wife, who was more gentle than most of her people, asked them to come in and rest, advising them to be ready to run when they should hear the giant coming, and to hide behind a row of kettles which hung from a beam at the back end of the hall. "For," said she, "my husband may be very angry when he finds strangers here, and often the glance of his eye is so fierce that it kills!"

At first the mighty Thor and brave Tyr were not willing to hide like cowards; but at last they agreed to the plan, upon the good wife promising to call them out as soon as she had told her husband about them.

It was not long before they heard the heavy steps of Hymir, as he came striding into his icy home; and very lucky it was for Thor and Tyr that the giantess had told them to hide, for when the giant heard that two of the Æsir from Asgard were in his home, so fierce a flash shot from his eyes that it broke the beam from which the kettles hung, and they all fell broken on the floor except Mile-deep.

After a while the giant grew quiet, and at last even began to be polite to his guests. He had been unlucky at his fishing that day, so he had to kill three of his oxen for supper. Thor being hungry, as usual, made Hymir quite angry by eating two whole oxen, so that, when they rose from the table the giant said, "If you keep on eating as much at every meal, as you have to-night, Thor, you will have to find your own food."

"Very well," said Thor; "I will go fishing with you in the morning!"

II.

Next morning Thor set forth with the giant, and as they walked over the fields toward the sea, Thor cut off the head of one of the finest oxen, for bait. Of course you may know that Hymir was not pleased at this, but Thor said he should need the very best kind of bait, for he was hoping to catch the Midgard serpent, that dangerous monster who lived at the bottom of the ocean, coiled around the world, with his tail in his mouth.

When they came to the shore where the boat was ready, each one took an oar, and they rowed out to deep water. Hymir was tired first, and called to Thor to stop. "We are far enough out!" he cried "This is my usual fishing-place, where I find the best whales. If we go farther the sea will be rougher, and we may run into the Midgard serpent."

As this was just what Thor wanted, he rowed all the harder, and did not stop until they were far out on the ocean; then he baited his hook with the ox's head, and threw it overboard. Soon there came a fierce jerk on the line; it grew heavier and heavier, but Thor pulled with all his might. He tugged so hard that he broke through the bottom of the boat, and had to stand on the slippery rocks beneath.

All this time the giant was looking on, wondering what was the matter, but when he saw the horrid head of the Midgard serpent rising above the waves, he was so frightened that he cut the line; and Thor, after trying so hard to rid the world of that dangerous monster, saw him fall back again under the water; even Miölnir, the magic hammer, which Thor hurled at the creature, was too late to hit him. And so the two fishermen had to turn back, and wade to the shore, carrying the broken boat and oars with them.

The giant was proud to think he had been too quick for Thor, and after they reached the house he said to the thunder-god, "Since you think you are so strong, let us see you break this goblet; if you succeed, I will give you the big kettle."

This was just what Thor wanted; so he tightened his belt of strength, and threw the goblet with all his might against the wall; but instead of breaking the goblet he broke the wall.

A second time he tried, but did no better. Then the giant's wife whispered to Thor, "Throw it at his head!" And she sang in a low voice, as she turned her spinning-wheel,—

"Hard the pillar, hard the stone,
Harder yet the giant's bone!
Stones shall break and pillars fall,
Hymir's forehead breaks them all!"

Yet again Thor threw the goblet, this time against the giant's head, and it fell, broken in pieces.

Then Tyr tried to lift the Mile-deep kettle, for he was in a hurry to leave this land of ice and snow; but he could not stir it from its place, and Thor had to help him, before they could get it out of the giant's house.

When Hymir saw the gods, whom he hated, carrying off his kettle, he called all his giant friends, and they started out in chase of the Æsir; but when Thor heard them coming he turned and saw their fierce, grinning faces glaring down at him from every rocky peak and iceberg.

Then the mighty Thunderer raised Miölnir, the hammer, above his head, and hurled it among the giants, who became stiff and cold, all turned into giant rocks, that still stand by the shore.

III.

Ægir was very glad to get Mile-deep; so he set to work to make the mead in it, to get ready for the great feast, at the time of the flax harvest, when all the Æsir were coming from Asgard to visit him.

Before the day came, all light and joy had gone from the sacred city, because the bright Baldur had been slain, and the homes of the gods were dark and lonely without him. So they were all glad to visit Ægir, to find cheer for their sadness.

There was Father Odin, with his golden helmet, and Queen Frigga, wearing her crown of stars, golden-haired Sif, Freyja, with Brisingamen, the wonderful necklace, and all the noble company of the Æsir, all except mighty Thor, who had gone far away to the giant-land.

As they all sat in Ægir's beautiful ocean hall, drinking the sweet mead, and talking together, Loki came in and stood before them; but, finding he was not welcome, and no seat saved for him, he began saying ugly things to make them all angry, and at last he grew angry himself, and slew Ægir's servant because they praised him. The Æsir drove him out from the hall, but once more he came in, and said such dreadful things that at last Frigga said, "Oh, if my son Baldur were only here, he would silence thy wicked tongue!"

Then Loki turned to Frigga, and told her that he himself was the very one who had slain Baldur. He had no sooner spoken than a heavy peal of thunder shook the hall, and angry Thor strode in, waving his magic hammer. Seeing this, the coward Loki turned and fled, and Asgard was rid of him forever.

THE PUNISHMENT OF LOKI.

When Loki was driven out by the mighty Thor from Ægir's palace-hall he knew that he could never again be allowed to come among the gods in Asgard. Many times had this mischievous fire-god brought trouble and sorrow to the Æsir, but now he had done the most cruel deed of all, he had slain Baldur the Good, and had driven all light and joy from Asgard.

Far away he fled, among the mountains, hoping that no one would find him there ; and near a lovely mountain stream he built for himself a hut with four doors looking north, east, south, and west, so that if the wise Allfather, on his high air throne in Asgard, should see him, and send messengers to punish him, the watchful Loki could see them coming and escape by the opposite door.

He spent most of the days and nights thinking how

he could get away from the Æsir. "If I ran to the stream and turned myself into a fish," he thought, "I wonder if they could catch me. I could keep out of the way of a hook; but then there are nets; Ægir's wife has a wonderful thing like a net, for catching fish, and that would be far worse than a hook!"

When Loki thought of the net, he began to wonder how it was made, and the more he thought, the more he wished he could make one so as to see how a fish could keep from getting caught in it. He sat down by the fire in his little hut, took a piece of cord and began to make a fish-net. He had nearly finished it when, looking up through the open door, he saw three of the Æsir in the distance, coming toward his hut. Loki well knew that they were coming to catch him, and, quickly throwing his net into the fire, he ran to the stream, changed himself into a beautiful spotted salmon, and leaped into the water.

A moment later the three gods entered the hut, and one of them spied the fish-net burning in the fire. "See!" cried he, "Loki must have been making this net to catch fish; he always was a good fisherman, and now this is just what we want for catching him!"

So they snatched the last bit of the net from the fire, and by looking at it found out how to make

THE PUNISHMENT OF LOKI.

another, which they took with them to the bank of the stream.

The first time the net was put into the water, Loki hid between two rocks, and the net was so light that it floated past him; but the next time it had a heavy stone weight, which made it sink down, till Loki saw he could not get away unless he could leap over the net. He did this, but Thor, seeing him, waded out into the stream, where he threw the net again, so that Loki must jump a second time, or else go on out into the deep sea.

As he leaped, Thor stooped and caught him in his hand, but the fish was so slippery that Thor could hardly hold it. In the struggle the salmon's tail was pinched so tightly by the thunder-god's strong fingers that it was drawn out to a point, and the old stories say that is why salmon tails are so pointed ever since.

Thus was Loki caught in his own trap, and dreadful was his punishment. The Æsir chained him to a high rock, and placed a great, poisonous serpent, hanging over the cliff above his head.

If it had not been for Loki's good, faithful wife, he would have died of the poison that dropped from the snake's mouth. She watched by her husband, holding a cup above him to catch the poison. Only when she had to turn aside to empty the cup did the drops fall upon Loki; then they gave him such terrible pain that he shook the earth with his struggles, and the people in Midgard fled from the dreadful earthquake, in Iceland the great geysers, springs of hot water, burst through the earth, and in the south-lands burning ashes and lava poured down the mountain-sides.

There, chained to the cliff, the cruel, mischievous Loki was to lie until the Twilight of the gods, the dark day of Ragnarök, when all the mighty evil monsters and beasts would get free, and the terrible battle be fought between them and the gods of Asgard.

THE TWILIGHT OF THE GODS.

LOKI and Fenrir, the wolf, were safely bound, each to his separate cliff, but still happiness and peace did not return to Asgard, for Baldur was no longer there, and light and joy had gone from the home of the gods. The Æsir felt that the Twilight of the gods, which Odin knew was to come, must be near.

Soon began a long cold winter; surely it must be the beginning of the Fimbulwinter, which was to come before the last great battle. From the north came cold blasts of freezing wind; snow and ice covered the earth; men could not see the face of the sun or the moon. Everywhere there was darkness; the people grew fierce and unhappy and wicked, for they seemed no longer to love each other. So the evil deeds of men kept on, and the fierce frost giants grew stronger and stronger.

They killed the trees and flowers, and bound the lakes and rivers with icy bands.

Even when summer time came, the cold still held on, and no one could see the green grass or the beautiful golden sunlight. The frost giants were pleased to see the trouble they had brought upon men, and hoped they soon could destroy Asgard and the gods.

Three long winters passed, with no light to warm and brighten the world; after that still three other dreary winters, and then the eagle who sat on the top of the great world tree, Yggdrasil, gave a loud, shrill cry; at that the earth shook, the rocks crumbled and fell, so that Loki and the wolf were freed from their chains.

The waters of the deep ocean rose and rolled high over the land, and up above the waves writhing out of the deep, came the monster Midgard serpent to join in the last battle. Now the enemies of the gods were gathering from all sides, — the frost giants, the mountain giants, with Loki, Fenrir, and the Midgard serpent.

Heimdall, the faithful watchman, looked from his watch-tower by the rainbow bridge, and when he saw the host of monsters appearing and raging toward Asgard, he blew his magic horn, Giallar, which was the signal of warning to the gods.

THOR FIGHTING THE SERPENT.

When Father Odin heard the blast of Heimdall's horn, he hastened to arm himself for the battle; once again it is said the Allfather sought wisdom at Mimir's fountain, asking to know how best to lead the Æsir against their enemies. But what Mimir said to him no one ever knew, for a second call sounded from the Giallar horn, and the gods, with Odin at their head, rode forth from Asgard to meet their foes.

Thor took his place beside Odin, but they were soon parted in the struggle. The thunder-god fell upon his old enemy, the serpent, whom twice before he had tried to slay, and after a fierce fight, he at last conquered and slew the monster; but the poisonous breath from the serpent's mouth overcame the mighty Thor, and he also fell.

Heimdall and Loki came face to face, and each slew the other. Thus every one of the gods battled each with his foe, till at last the darkness grew deeper, and all, both gods and giants lay dead. Then fire burst forth, raging from Utgard to Asgard—and all the worlds were destroyed in that dreadful day of Ragnarök.

But this was not the end of all: after many months, and years, and even centuries had passed, a new world began to appear, with the fair ocean, and the beautiful land, with a bright, shining sun by day, and the moon and stars by night. Then once more the light and heat from the sun made the grass and trees grow, and the flowers bloom.

Baldur and Hodur came to this beautiful new world, and walked and talked together. Thor's sons were there, too, and with them, the hammer, Miölnir, no longer for use against giants, but for helping men build homes.

Two people, a man and a woman, who were kept safe through the raging fire, now came to dwell on the earth, and all their children and grandchildren lived at peace with each other in this beautiful new world.

Baldur and Hodur talked often of the old days when the Æsir dwelt in Asgard, before Loki, the wicked one, brought darkness and trouble to them. With loving words they spoke of Odin and Frigga; and the brave Tyr, who gave his right hand to save the Æsir; of mighty Thor; and faithful Heimdall; of lovely Freyja, with her beautiful necklace; and of fair Iduna's garden, where they used to sit and eat her magic apples. "But still," they said, "we know now that this new world is fairer than the old, and here, also, the loving Allfather watches over his children."

INDEX OF NAMES.

Ægir (ā'jir). God of the deep sea.
Æsir (ā'sir). The twelve gods of Asgard.
Alfheim (ălf'hīm). Home of the elves and of Frey.
Asgard (as'gärd). The home of the Æsir.
Baldur (bąl'der). The sun-god.
Bifröst (bē'frĕst). The rainbow bridge.
Bragi (brä'gē). The god of poetry. Husband of Iduna.
Brisingamen (brī sing'ä men). Freyja's necklace.
Brock. One of the dwarfs.
Fenrir. The monster wolf.
Fimbulwinter (fim'bul). The last stormy winter.
Frey (frī). The god of summer and of the elves.
Freyja (frī'yă). The goddess of love and beauty.
Frigga (frĭg'ä). The queen of the gods. Wife of Odin.
Giallar-Horn (Gyäl'lar). Heimdall's trumpet.
Gladsheim (glădz'hīm). Odin's palace.
Heimdall (hīm'däl). Guardian of the rainbow bridge.
Hela (hē'lä). Queen of the underworld.
Hermod (hĕr'mod). The messenger-god.
Hodur (ho'der). God of darkness. Baldur's brother.
Hönir (hĕ'nir). God of mind or thought.
Hymir (hē'mir). The frost giant who owned the great kettle called Mile-deep.
Iduna (ē doon'ä). Goddess of spring.
Jötunheim (yĕ'toon hīm). Home of the giants.
Loki (lō'kē). God of fire.
Midgard. The earth.
Mimir (mē'mir). Guardian of the well of wisdom.
Miölnir (myĕl'nir). Thor's magic hammer.

Niflheim (nĭfl'hīm). The underground world.
Niörd (nyẽrd). God of the seashore.
Norns. The three Fates.
Odin (ō'din). The father, or chief, of the gods.
Odur (ō'dûr). Freyja's husband.
Ragnarök (råg'nå rûk). The Twilight of the gods.
Sif. Wife of Thor.
Sindri. One of the dwarfs.
Skadi (skä'dē). Thiassi's daughter.
Sleipnir (slīp'nir). Odin's eight-footed steed.
Thiassi (tē äs'sē). A frost giant. Skadi's father.
Thor (thor or tor). God of thunder.
Tyr (tēr) or **Tiu** (tū). God of war.
Utgard (ōōt'gärd). City of the giants, in Jötunheim.
Yggdrasil (ig'drå sil). The world tree.

KEY TO PRONUNCIATION.

ā *as in* ale. ạ *as in* all. ẽ *as in* fern.
ă *as in* am. å *as in* ask. ī *as in* ice.
ä *as in* arm. ē *as in* eve. ĭ *as in* ill.
ō *as in* old. û *as in* urn.
ōō *as in* foot. ū *as in* use.